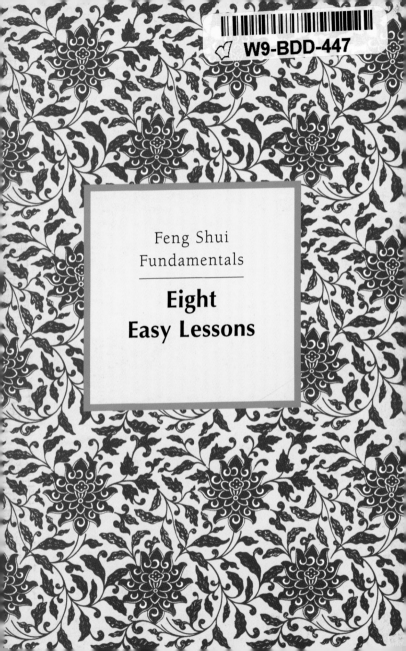

W9-BDD-447

Feng Shui
Fundamentals

Eight
Easy Lessons

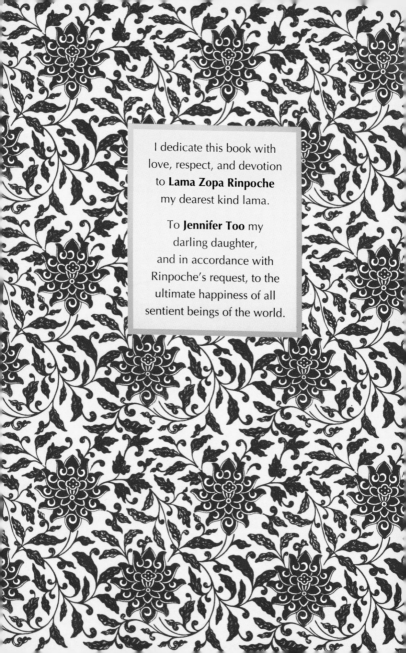

I dedicate this book with
love, respect, and devotion
to **Lama Zopa Rinpoche**
my dearest kind lama.

To **Jennifer Too** my
darling daughter,
and in accordance with
Rinpoche's request, to the
ultimate happiness of all
sentient beings of the world.

Feng Shui
Fundamentals

Eight Easy Lessons

Lillian Too

BARNES
&NOBLE
BOOKS
NEW YORK

© Element Books Limited 1997
Text © Lillian Too 1997

This edition published by
BARNES & NOBLE INC.
by arrangement with
ELEMENT BOOKS LIMITED

1997 BARNES & NOBLE BOOKS

Designed and created with
THE BRIDGEWATER BOOK COMPANY LIMITED

ELEMENT BOOKS LIMITED
Editorial Director Julia McCutchen
Managing Editor Caro Ness
Production Director Roger Lane
Production Sarah Golden

THE BRIDGEWATER BOOK COMPANY LIMITED
Art Director Terry Jeavons
Designer James Lawrence
Managing Editor Anne Townley
Project Editor Andrew Kirk
Editor Linda Doeser
Picture Research Julia Hanson
Studio Photography Guy Ryecart
Illustrations Isabel Rayner, Andrew Kulman, Mark Jamieson,
Michaela Blunden, Paul Collicutt, Olivia Rayner, Jackie Harland

Printed and bound in Hong Kong

ISBN 0 7607 1878 4

The publishers wish to thank the following for the use of pictures:
Elizabeth Whiting Associates, pp 14, 16; Julia Hanson, pp 13, 47; Image Bank, pp 9, 33, 42, 44;
and Zefa, pp 9, 11, 15, 45, 47, 57.

Special thanks go to:
Bright Ideas, Lewes, East Sussex
for help with properties

Lillian Too's website addresses are
http://www.asiaconnect.com.my/lillian-too
http://www.dragonmagic.com

Lillian Too's email addresses are
ltoo@dragonmagic.com
ltoo@popmail.asiaconnect.com.my

CONTENTS

THE CHINESE VIEW OF THE LIVING EARTH

THE WINDS AND THE WATERS

風水

Feng shui means "wind and water." In the literal sense it refers to the topography of the earth: its mountains, valleys, and waterways, whose shapes and sizes, orientation, and levels, are created by the continuous interaction of these two powerful forces of nature.

To people of Chinese origin all over the world, feng shui connotes a mystical practice that blends ancient wisdom with cultural superstitions. This broad body of traditional knowledge lays down guidelines for differentiating between auspicious and inauspicious land sites. It also provides instructions on how to orient homes and design room layouts to enhance the quality of life dramatically.

In the family home, well-oriented feng shui features work to create harmonious relationships between husband and wife and between children and parents, foster good health, and attract abundance and prosperity. They bring good fortune to the breadwinner, build good reputations, and strengthen descendants' luck – children who will bring honor and happiness to the family in the future .

In business premises, good feng shui creates opportunities for growth, elevates prestige in the community, attracts customers, raises profits, and expands turnover. Employees stay loyal and a pervasive aura of goodwill ensures smooth working relationships.

Good feng shui results when the winds and the waters surrounding your home and work space are harmonious and well balanced. Bad feng shui, on the other hand, brings illness, disasters, accidents, burglaries, and financial loss. It results in lost opportunities, fading careers, squandered wealth, and collapsed reputations. Above all, bad feng shui causes grave unhappiness, and it can sometimes even provoke tragic consequences for the reputation and well-being of the family unit as a whole.

WHAT IS FENG SHUI?

Feng shui advocates living in harmony with the earth's environment and energy lines so that there is balance with the forces of nature.

Feng shui contends that the environment is crowded with powerful, but invisible, energy lines.

Feng shui says that some of these energy lines are auspicious, bringing great good fortune, while some are pernicious and hostile, bringing death and the destruction of happiness.

Feng shui offers ways of arranging the home so that these energy lines become harmonious and bring prosperity and harmony, rather than loss and discord.

Good feng shui practice encourages good luck to flow through your home and touch all who live there, just as this meandering river flowing through the landscape nourishes the surrounding farmland.

Positive energy would have difficulty accumulating in this barren, windswept landscape.

Feng shui instructs us in the clever harnessing of auspicious energy lines – generally referred to as sheng chi, the dragon's cosmic breath – making sure they meander gently through the home and accumulate and settle, thereby bringing good fortune.

Feng shui teaches us to avoid, deflect, and dissolve inauspicious energy lines – also known as shar chi – which represent the killing breath caused by secret poison arrows in the surroundings.

Feng shui strenuously warns against sleeping, working, sitting, eating, and generally living in places that are hit by these pernicious hostile energy lines.

THE LANDSCAPES OF THE WORLD

Feng shui is an exciting component of ancient Chinese wisdom – a science that goes back at least 4,000 years to the days of the emperors and mythical legends. That it has so brilliantly survived the centuries bears testimony to its potency. In recent years there has been an extensive revival of interest in its practice, particularly in the West, where the study of feng shui began as a New Age phenomenon, but has now attracted mainstream attention.

The current popularity of feng shui stems from the widespread appeal of its simple logic. While its many theories and guidelines are based on the Chinese view of the universe, the fundamentals are easily understood and widely applicable. Its laws and tenets relate to simple basic concepts that advocate living harmoniously with the environment, creating balance in the living space, and blending in with the natural landscapes of the world: the contours of the land, the terrain of the earth, the rivers, and waterways of the world, sunlight and moonlight, vegetation, orientations, and directions – in short, the winds and waters of the living earth that surrounds us.

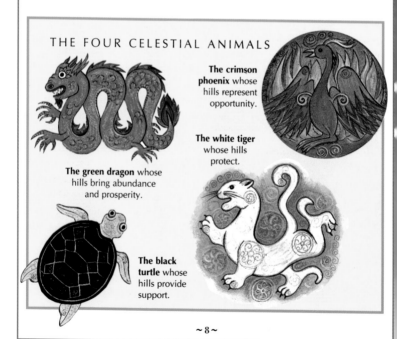

THE FOUR CELESTIAL ANIMALS

The crimson phoenix whose hills represent opportunity.

The white tiger whose hills protect.

The green dragon whose hills bring abundance and prosperity.

The black turtle whose hills provide support.

CLASSICAL FENG SHUI

A fundamental tenet of feng shui advises you to live with your back to a mountain. So if your home is backed by something solid and firm, such as a hill or a building that simulates the hill, you will have support all your life. Thus the first part of classical feng shui is to have the mountain behind.

There should be open space in front of your home, so that your vision is not hampered and your horizon is visible. If there is also a view of water, it brings auspicious energy into your living area. Moreover, if the river is slow moving and meandering, the good energy has a chance to settle and accumulate before entering your home, thereby allowing you to partake of its essence. Needless to say, the cleaner, fresher, and more sparkling the

This house, safely nestled among protective undulating green hills, enjoys the support of mountains in the background and the auspicious energy of nearby water.

water, the greater the good fortune that it will bring. Thus, the second half of classical feng shui says have water in front of your home.

In the lyrical language of the ancients, this classical feng shui configuration describes the mountain behind as the black turtle hills and the river in front, with its footstool of a hillock, as the phoenix hills. On the left, feng shui introduces the important green dragon, a range of hills that is gentle and undulating, while on the right are the lower white tiger hills. The symbolism of these four celestial animals describes classical feng shui landscape configuration. If your home is comfortably nestled within the bosom of these four animals, you will be supported by the black turtle, made prosperous by the green dragon, protected by the white tiger, and brought wonderful opportunities by the crimson phoenix.

The optimum feng shui configuration looking from the house:
black turtle hills behind for support; the crimson phoenix hill in front for good luck; the green dragon hills, on the left for prosperity; and smaller hills, the white tiger, on the right for protection.

THE FUNDAMENTALS
OF FENG SHUI

THE HARMONY
OF YIN AND YANG ENERGIES

At its most basic, feng shui is a question of balance, but this balance is related to the complementarity of opposites, expressed in terms of the yin and the yang. According to the Chinese, all things in the universe are either the female yin or the male yang, the dark yin or the bright yang.

Yin and yang together make up the wholeness of the universe, which includes heaven and earth. Yin and yang breathe meaning into each other, for without one, the other cannot exist. Thus, without the yin of darkness, there cannot be the light of yang, without the cold temperature of yin, there cannot possibly be the warmth of yang – and vice versa.

When there is balance between the yin and yang, the wholeness of the universe is represented. There is good balance and prosperity, health, well-being, and happiness. Feng shui practice always includes a yin-yang analysis of room space, land configurations, sunlight and shade, dampness and dryness, bright and pale colors, and solids and fluids. Rooms that are too yin are not auspicious; there are insufficient life energies to bring prosperity. Rooms that are too yang are said to be damaging because there is too much energy, causing accidents and huge losses. Only rooms – and homes – with balanced yin and yang can be auspicious and will be made even more auspicious if there is a good balance of yin and yang outside.

The ancient Chinese symbol of yin and yang represents the delicate interplay of complementary opposites that underpins the structure of the whole universe.

Graveyards, and other places associated with death, are full of strong yin energy that is passed on to nearby houses and buildings.

HOMES THAT ARE TOO YIN

Houses and buildings built too near graveyards, hospitals, prisons, slaughter-houses, and police stations are too yin because such places are associated with the yin energies of death. Even places of worship, such as temples, churches, and mosques, are said to give out extreme yin energies because of the rituals associated with mourning held there. The same diagnosis is often pronounced on buildings that are located on land that previously housed these places making it advisable to research the history of your home.

REMEDIES

It is better to avoid living in such yin places, but if you really cannot help it, then there are some remedies.

- ▓ Orient your main door so that it faces away from the yin structure or building.
- ▓ Do not have windows that open toward these yin structures.
- ▓ Paint your door bright red to signify strong, powerful yang energy.
- ▓ Make sure your porch is always well lit. Keep the light on all the time.
- ▓ Bring in the yang sunlight by cutting back shady trees.
- ▓ Plant trees with luscious vegetation and grow flowers in the garden.
- ▓ Put garden lights all round the house.
- ▓ Paint your fence a bright, happy color.
- ▓ Make sure you have a red roof.
- ▓ Introduce yang objects, such as boulders, pebbles, and stones, into the garden.

Large, unobstructed windows help to dissipate the excess yin energy that can accumulate in small, cramped rooms.

ROOMS THAT ARE TOO YIN

Rooms that never see sunlight, are damp, decorated in only shades of gray and blue, narrow and cramped, always closed and silent, or which have been occupied for a long time by someone who has been chronically sick, have too much yin energy. They cause sickness and bad luck to befall the residents. People who stay in rooms that have an excess of yin energy suffer more than their fair share of misfortunes and seem to be shrouded by a cloak of ill luck.

CREATING YANG ENERGY

Try to create some yang energy by doing the following.

- Repaint the walls with a bright yang color – pinks, yellows, even red.
- Bring in the light. White walls are very yang because they are bright.
- Throw away draping curtains and bring the sunlight into the room.
- Use happy colors for your curtains.
- Use bright colors for duvets, bed sheets and other soft furnishings.

- Keep the windows open.
- If trees are blocking the light from outside, cut them back.
- Install plenty of lights and keep at least one turned on continuously.
- Keep the radio or television turned on. Sound, life, and laughter bring in yang energy.
- Have vases of freshly cut flowers.
- Introduce movement with mobiles and wind chimes. They symbolize life energy.

Electrical transmission pylons and overhead wires can overwhelm homes with too much yang energy.

HOMES THAT ARE TOO YANG

Buildings that are constantly exposed to bright sunlight or heat of any kind are said to have an excess of yang energy, to the extent that it brings accidents, disasters, and grave misfortune. If you are living too near an electrical transmitter, or you are within view of large factory or refinery chimneys that belch noxious smoke throughout the day, there is too much yang energy.

It is advisable to move from such a place, but if you have no choice, then it is necessary – indeed vital – that you combat the excess yang energy by introducing yin structures or surround yourself with the colors and characteristics of yin. Water is one of the best cures for too much yang energy; creating a small pond of water in the garden will effectively counter the yang energy.

REMEDIES

Remedies for too much yang energy.

- Paint your door in any shade of blue, as this is a yin color.
- Select muted, cool colors for your interior decor.
- Avoid too much noise in the house.
- Avoid too much light in the house, and never have a red light turned on.
- Introduce water features, such as miniature fountains.
- Hang paintings of lakes and rivers in your home.
- Maintain a good lawn in your garden.
- Paint railings and gates black, as this, too, is a yin color.

ROOMS THAT ARE TOO YANG

If you play loud music all day long and your room is fitted with bright red furnishings and the walls are painted red or bright yellow, the energies are too yang. There is too much noise and too much energy, so you would be well advised to introduce some yin features to counter this imbalance. Observe some periods of silence during the day. Change your drapes to a darker yin color or even install a blue light.

This black and white color scheme creates a harmony of opposites.

Similarly, if your room receives direct hot afternoon sun, the room is too yang. Counter this by hanging some heavier drapes that cut out the glare of the sun. Or hang a faceted crystal that transforms the hostile sunlight into the bright colors of the rainbow, bringing in friendly yang energy rather than killing yang energy. Observe that creating a balance of yin and yang in your home is an extremely subtle exercise.

Essentially, a room should have elements of yin and yang but never too much of one or the other. Have music and life in the room, but not all the time. Have peace and quiet in the room, but not to the extent it becomes lifeless. Have a cool decor of blues and grays, but also incorporate a splash of yang color which may be represented by a vase of red roses or a painting of a sunrise.

Black and white color schemes are symbolic of yin and yang harmony, but there should also be sounds and life. A completely black and white decor that is always silent is regarded as much too yin in the same way that if there is too much noise, it is regarded as too yang.

Remember that feng shui is a subtle blend of opposite energies that complement each other. What you should always strive for is the harmony of opposites. This is the fundamental guiding principle of yin and yang.

THE EIGHT-SIDED PA KUA SYMBOL

This is probably the most important symbol of feng shui. The eight sides represent many things in the practice of feng shui, and by itself, it is also believed to symbolize powerful protective energies. Chinese people around the world hang the Pa Kua, above their main doors just outside their homes to guard against any killing energy that may inadvertently be shooting at them. This is usually caused by hostile objects or structures that represent poison arrows (see pages 40–47).

In the vocabulary of feng shui, the Pa Kua used as a protective symbol is the Pa Kua of the Early Heaven Arrangement. This has the trigrams arranged around the eight sides in a different way from the Pa Kua of the Later Heaven Arrangement. (see illustrations). The Early Heaven Pa Kua is also used in the practice of yin feng shui – the feng shui of grave sites for one's ancestors. The Chinese believe that the luck of descendants is hugely affected by the feng shui of their ancestors' graves.

For yang feng shui – the feng shui of the dwellings of the living, which is what concerns most of us – the symbol of the Later Heaven Pa Kua is significant. Here the arrangement of the trigrams around the eight sides gives meaning to the eight major directions of the compass represented on the Pa Kua, with south always placed at the top. It allows for the correct interpretation and relationships of the other symbols of feng shui.

These other symbols are associated with numbers (one to nine), the five elements (water, fire, earth, wood, and metal), the members of the family (father, mother, sons, and daughters), the celestial animals (turtle, dragon, tiger, and phoenix), and the characteristics of each of the eight trigrams themselves.

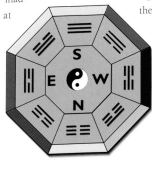

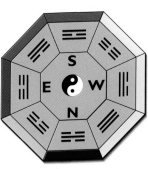

The Pa Kua of the Early Heaven Arrangement (above) and of the Later Heaven Arrangement (below).

THE EIGHT TRIGRAMS AROUND THE PA KUA

Chien is probably the most powerful of the eight trigrams. This symbol of three solid unbroken lines represents heaven, the patriarch, the leader, and the father. In the Pa Kua it is placed northwest in the Later Heaven Arrangement. Consequently, the northwest is said to represent the patriarch or the person from whom all power emanates. For yang dwellings, houses of the living, the power of the household is said to come from the northwest and hence this is the location of the head of the household. This trigram is yang.

Kun is the archetype of the maternal or mother earth. This is the symbol of yielding, represented by three broken yin lines. It is thus completely yin. In the Pa Kua it is placed southwest and it signifies all things female – domesticity, docility, and maternal instincts. The matriarch of the family is best placed in the southwest for all her noblest qualities to flourish and for it to bring good fortune to the family.

Chen, two broken yin lines above a solid yang line, is the trigram placed east in the arrangement around the Pa Kua. It signifies the season of spring, the quality of growth, and embodies the spirit of the first male descendant. In the palaces of the Chinese emperors in Beijing's Forbidden City, the male heirs to the throne resided in the east of the palace complex. In any home this, too, is where the eldest son of the family should reside.

Sun, two solid yang lines above a broken yin line, is the trigram that embodies the spirit of the eldest daughter. Located in the southeast, it also signifies the wood element and the virtue of gentleness. The wind that brings prosperity is also located in the southeast.

Ken signifies stillness, the mountain. Represented by two broken yin lines lying just beneath the surface of the solid yang line, this trigram also denotes a place of preparation. Here, too, the place of the youngest son is symbolized.
The location is northeast.

Kan also spells danger. Placed north, this trigram comprises a single solid yang line, surrounded by two broken yin lines, which signify the warmth of yang trapped by the cold of yin. Thus, Kan signifies winter and symbolizes water within which things are hidden. Kan represents the second son of the family.

Tui is the symbol of joyousness, represented by two solid yang lines about to break through the single yin line above. The season is fall, the direction is west and it represents the lake. The family member represented is the youngest daughter, who brings much joy and pleasure.

Li is placed in the south, opposite Kan. Here two solid yang lines trap the broken yin line, signifying the triumph of yang over yin. The element of this trigram is fire and the season is summer. Li signifies the brightness and beauty of summer. It is a trigram full of hope and it signifies the second daughter.

THE FIVE ELEMENTS

A core concept of feng shui practice is the theory of the five elements and their productive and destructive cycles. All Chinese astrological sciences, acupuncture, physical exercises such as chi kung, and medicine depend on an understanding of this theory for diagnosis and cures. In feng shui, understanding the nature and cycles of the elements vividly enhances the potency of its practice. This is because the Chinese view all things in the universe as belonging to one of the element groups. As each compass direction has its own ruling element, every corner of every home or room is also deemed to belong to one of these elements. The five elements are wood, fire, water, metal, and earth.

Feng shui practice takes account of element relationships by ensuring that the elements of objects, directions, and locations in any room do not destroy each other. Element relationships, based on their productive and destructive cycles, must, therefore, always be taken into account when any feng shui diagnosis or cure is being considered.

THE ELEMENTS

FIRE is red, considered a very auspicious yang color. Its season is summer and its direction is south. Symbols of this element are bright lights. Its number is nine. Fire animals are the snake and the horse.

WOOD is represented by all shades of green. Its season is spring. Big wood lies in the east, while small wood is in the southeast. Symbols of the wood element are plants, paper, furniture, and all things made of wood. In numerology, wood is represented by the numbers three and four. The Chinese horoscope lists the tiger and the rabbit as wood animals.

WATER is blue or black. Its season is winter and its direction is north. This is a yin element and its number is one. Objects that represent water include aquariums and fountains. Animals belonging to this element are the rat and the boar.

PRODUCTIVE AND DESTRUCTIVE CYCLES

PRODUCTIVE CYCLE
Each element creates the next in the cycle

WOOD · FIRE · EARTH · METAL · WATER

DESTRUCTIVE CYCLE
Each element destroys the next in the cycle

WOOD · EARTH · WATER · FIRE · METAL

In the productive cycle of the elements, fire produces earth, which creates metal, which makes water, which produces wood, which makes fire.

In the destructive cycle of elements, wood devours earth, which destroys water, which extinguishes fire, which consumes metal, which demolishes wood.

Try superimposing the destructive cycle of the elements above right on to the productive cycle above left. Start with wood at the top, move to earth below, up to water, across to fire, down to metal and back up to wood. You will find that you draw a five pointed star on to the productive cycle similar to the pentacle symbol of many ancient spiritual and religious practices.

METAL is signified by the metallic colors, gold or silver, and also white. Its season is fall and its directions are west (small metal) and northwest (big metal). Objects of the element are wind chimes, bells, coins, and jewelry. Its numbers are six and seven. The metal animals of the Chinese horoscope are the rooster and the monkey.

EARTH is represented by all shades of brown. It is the element of the center and it represents every third month of every season. Its directions are southwest (big earth) and northeast (small earth). Its numbers are two, five, and eight and its horoscope animals are the ox, the dragon, the sheep, and the dog.

THE LO SHU SQUARE AND THE MAGIC OF NUMBERS

The Lo Shu square is another important symbol widely used in feng shui analysis, especially in the application of various compass feng shui formulas.

This nine-sector grid features a unique arrangement of the numbers one to nine. This arrangement is deemed to be magical because the sum of three numbers in any direction in the square – horizontally, vertically, or diagonally – is 15, the number of days taken for a new moon to reach full moon. The Lo Shu square is, therefore, particularly significant in the time dimension of feng shui, supplementing the space dimension of general feng shui practice.

The three-grid pattern corresponds to the eight sides of the Pa Kua symbol, around a ninth central point. Like the Pa Kua, the direction south is placed at the top so that the number nine also corresponds to the direction south. The pattern of numbers is thus associated with the eight trigrams of the Pa Kua symbol when it is configured according to the Later Heaven Arrangement.

Feng shui practice bases many of its recommendations on the interpretation of

THE MAGIC SQUARE

Add up the numbers on the Lo Shu square in any direction and the result is always fifteen.

the relationships between the numbers of the Lo Shu square and the symbols of the Pa Kua. These emblems, therefore, exert a powerful and almost mythical influence on all aspects of Chinese cultural symbolism and their various attributes make up much of the underlying basis of feng shui practice today. This is because veteran practitioners in Taiwan, Hong Kong, Singapore, Malaysia, and elsewhere have discovered that the potency of these symbols remains undiminished when correctly applied to the orientation and architecture of modern buildings, towns, and cities.

The Lo Shu square of magic numbers superimposed on the back of the turtle – one of the four celestial animals.

There are striking similarities between the sequence of numbers on the Lo Shu square and symbols from other cultures, especially the Hebrew sign for the planet Saturn.

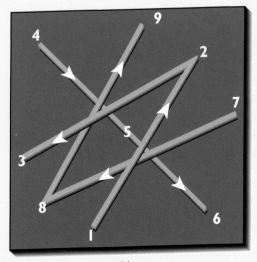

THE TOOLS OF FENG SHUI PRACTICE

DEMYSTIFYING THE LUO PAN COMPASS

風
水

The feng shui compass is known as the Luo Pan. In the center is the actual compass which, like the western compass, has its needle pointed to the magnetic north. However, unlike Western convention, Chinese feng shui practitioners make their analysis using south as the benchmark.

Ancient texts on the subject place south at the top and feng shui symbols also correspond to south being at the top. In practice however, the Chinese direction south is exactly the same as the south referred to by people in the West. Similarly, the Chinese direction north is exactly the same magnetic north used in the West. It is thus not necessary to use a Chinese feng shui Luo Pan. Any good Western compass is perfectly adequate. Equally, it is not necessary to transpose the directions. Whether you live in the northern or southern hemisphere, and whether you live in the East or the West, all directions referred to are the actual, real directions as indicated by an ordinary, modern compass.

The Luo Pan is a reference tool used by feng shui masters, and veterans of the science usually have their own versions of the Luo Pan containing summaries of their own notes and interpretations. These notes are jealously guarded as trade secrets and are placed in code in concentric rings around the compass. As the rings get larger, the meanings get deeper and refer to more advanced formulas. It is sufficient for the amateur practitioner to understand the

Any western compass can be used instead of the Luo Pan.

The first few rings of the Luo Pan show the relationship between the different symbols employed in feng shui practice.

first few inner rings of the compass and their meanings are illustrated here for easy reference.

When studying the feng shui compass, note that advanced feng shui uses secret formulas that examine the directions of doors, the flow of water, and the orientation of houses. These formulas divide each of the eight directions into three sub-directions, thereby offering different recommendations for each of 24 possible directions. Formula feng shui requires very precise and careful measurements of compass directions.

THE CHINESE CALENDAR

An important aspect of feng shui practice uses a person's date of birth and ruling year elements to determine the suitability of directions for doors and orientation for sleeping and working. Use the calendar here to convert Western birth dates into the equivalent Chinese dates for later analysis of Kua numbers. Take note of your birth year element, as this lets you know which elements will be auspicious for you.

Year	From	To	Element	Year	From	To	Element
1900	31 Jan 1900	18 Feb 1901	Metal	1923	16 Feb 1923	4 Feb 1924	Water
1901	19 Feb 1901	17 Feb 1902	Metal	1924	5 Feb 1924	24 Jan 1925	Wood
1902	8 Feb 1902	28 Jan 1903	Water	1925	25 Jan 1925	12 Feb 1926	Wood
1903	29 Jan 1903	15 Jan 1904	Water	1926	13 Feb 1926	1 Feb 1927	Fire
1904	16 Feb 1904	3 Feb 1905	Wood	1927	2 Feb 1927	22 Jan 1928	Fire
1905	4 Feb 1905	24 Jan 1906	Wood	1928	23 Jan 1928	9 Feb 1929	Earth
1906	25 Jan 1906	12 Feb 1907	Fire	1929	10 Feb 1929	29 Jan 1930	Earth
1907	13 Feb 1907	1 Feb 1908	Fire	1930	30 Jan 1930	16 Feb 1931	Metal
1908	2 Feb 1908	21 Jan 1909	Earth	1931	17 Feb 1931	15 Feb 1932	Metal
1909	22 Jan 1909	9 Feb 1910	Earth	1932	6 Feb 1932	25 Jan 1933	Water
1910	10 Feb 1910	29 Jan 1911	Metal	1933	26 Jan 1933	13 Feb 1934	Water
1911	30 Jan 1911	17 Feb 1912	Metal	1934	14 Feb 1934	3 Feb 1935	Wood
1912	18 Feb 1912	25 Feb 1913	Water	1935	4 Feb 1935	23 Jan 1936	Wood
1913	6 Feb 1913	25 Jan 1914	Water	1936	24 Jan 1936	10 Feb 1937	Fire
1914	26 Jan 1914	13 Feb 1915	Wood	1937	11 Feb 1937	30 Jan 1938	Fire
1915	14 Feb 1915	2 Feb 1916	Wood	1938	31 Jan 1938	18 Feby 1939	Earth
1916	3 Feb 1916	22 Jan 1917	Fire	1939	19 Feb 1939	7 Feb 1940	Earth
1917	23 Jan 1917	10 Feb 1918	Fire	1940	8 Feb 1940	26 Jan 1941	Metal
1918	11 Feb 1918	31 Jan 1919	Earth	1941	27 Jan 1941	14 Feb 1942	Metal
1919	1 Feb 1919	19 Feb 1920	Earth	1942	15 Feb 1942	24 Feb 1943	Water
1920	20 Feb 1920	7 Feb 1921	Metal	1943	5 Feb 1943	24 Jan 1944	Water
1921	8 Feb 1921	27 Jan 1922	Metal	1944	25 Jan 1944	12 Feb 1945	Wood
1922	28 Jan 1922	15 Feb 1923	Water	1945	13 Feb 1945	1 Feb 1946	Wood

Year	From	To	Element	Year	From	To	Element
1946	2 Feb 1946	21 Jan 1947	Fire	1977	18 Feb 1977	6 Feb 1978	Fire
1947	22 Jan 1947	9 Feb 1948	Fire	1978	7 Feb 1978	27 Jan 1979	Earth
1948	10 Feb 1948	28 Jan 1949	Earth	1979	28 Jan 1979	15 Feb 1980	Earth
1949	29 Jan 1949	16 Feb 1950	Earth	1980	16 Feb 1980	4 Feb 1981	Metal
1950	17 Feb 1950	5 Feb 1951	Metal	1981	5 Feb 1981	24 Jan 1982	Metal
1951	6 Feb 1951	26 Jan 1952	Metal	1982	25 Jan 1982	12 Feb 1983	Water
1952	27 Jan 1952	13 Feb 1953	Water	1983	13 Feb 1983	1 Feb 1984	Water
1953	14 Feb 1953	2 Feb 1954	Water	1984	2 Feb 1984	19 Feb 1985	Wood
1954	3 Feb 1954	23 Jan 1955	Wood	1985	20 Feb 1985	8 Feb 1986	Wood
1955	24 Jan 1955	11 Feb 1956	Wood	1986	9 Feb 1986	28 Jan 1987	Fire
1956	12 Feb 1956	30 Jan 1957	Fire	1987	29 Jan 1987	16 Feb 1988	Fire
1957	31 Jan 1957	17 Feb 1958	Fire	1988	17 Feb 1988	5 Feb 1989	Earth
1958	18 Feb 1958	7 Feb 1959	Earth	1989	6 Feb 1989	26 Jan 1990	Earth
1959	8 Feb 1959	27 Jan 1960	Earth	1990	27 Jan 1990	14 Feb 1991	Metal
1960	28 Jan 1960	14 Feb 1961	Metal	1991	15 Feb 1991	3 Feb 1992	Metal
1961	15 Feb 1961	4 Feb 1962	Metal	1992	4 Feb 1992	22 Jan 1993	Water
1962	5 Feb 1962	24 Jan 1963	Water	1993	23 Jan 1993	9 Feb 1994	Water
1963	25 Jan 1963	12 Feb 1964	Water	1994	10 Feb 1994	30 Jan 1995	Wood
1964	13 Feb 1964	1 Feb 1965	Wood	1995	31 Jan 1995	18 Feb 1996	Wood
1965	2 Feb 1965	20 Jan 1966	Wood	1996	19 Feb 1996	7 Feb 1997	Fire
1966	21 Jan 1966	8 Feb 1967	Fire	1997	8 Feb 1997	27 Jan 1998	Fire
1967	9 Feb 1967	29 Jan 1968	Fire	1998	28 Jan 1998	15 Feb 1999	Earth
1968	30 Jan 1968	16 Feb 1969	Earth	1999	16 Feb 1999	4 Feb 2000	Earth
1969	17 Feb 1969	5 Feb 1970	Earth	2000	5 Feb 2000	23 Jan 2001	Metal
1970	6 Feb 1970	26 Jan 1971	Metal	2001	24 Jan 2001	11 Feb 2002	Metal
1971	27 Jan 1971	15 Feb 1972	Metal	2002	12 Feb 2002	31 Jan 2003	Water
1972	16 Feb 1972	22 Jan 1973	Water	2003	1 Feb 2003	21 Jan 2004	Water
1973	3 Feb 1973	22 Jan 1974	Water	2004	22 Jan 2004	8 Feb 2005	Wood
1974	23 Jan 1974	10 Feb 1975	Wood	2005	9 Feb 2005	28 Jan 2006	Wood
1975	11 Feb 1975	30 Jan 1976	Wood	2006	29 Jan 2006	17 Feb 2007	Fire
1976	31 Jan 1976	17 Feb 1977	Fire	2007	18 Feb 2007	6 Feb 2008	Fire

THE FENG SHUI RULER

There are auspicious and inauspicious dimensions and most Chinese carpenters possess something called the feng shui ruler, which allows them to see at a glance whether the tables, closets, windows, and doors that they are making have acceptable dimensions.

The feng shui measuring tape has eight cycles of dimensions, four of which are auspicious and four inauspicious. Each cycle measures the equivalent of

AUSPICIOUS DIMENSIONS

CHAI: this is the first segment of the cycle and is subdivided into four categories of good luck, each approximately ½in or 13mm. The first brings money luck, the second brings a safe filled with jewels, the third brings together six types of good luck, while the fourth brings abundance. (Chai: 0–2⅛ins, 0–54mm.)

YI: this is the fourth segment of the cycle. It brings mentor luck, that is, it attracts helpful people into your life. The first sub-section means luck with children, the second predicts unexpected added income, the third predicts a very successful son, and the fourth offers good fortune. (Yi: 6⅜–8½ins, 162–215mm.)

KWAN: this third set of auspicious dimensions bring power luck and is similarly divided into four sub-sections. The first sub-sector means ease in passing exams, the second predicts special or speculative luck, the third offers improved income, while the fourth attracts high honors for the family. (Kwan: 8½–10⅝ins, 215–270mm.)

PUN: this fourth set of auspicious dimensions is divided into four sub-sections like the others. The first sub-sector bring lots of money flowing in, the next spells good luck in examinations, the third predicts plenty of jewelry, and the fourth sub-sector offers abundant prosperity. (Pun: 14¾in–17ins, 375–432mm.)

17 inches or 432mm, and each cycle is categorized into eight sections. The cycle of lucky and unlucky dimensions then repeats itself continuously. Once you have familiarized yourself with the use of the feng shui ruler, you can apply it to almost everything measurable to tap into the auspicious dimensions. In addition to furniture, doors, and windows, you can also use it on calling cards, envelopes, notepads or memo paper.

INAUSPICIOUS DIMENSIONS

PI: this category of bad luck refers to sickness. It also has four sub-sectors, each approximately 1/2in or 13mm. The first carries the meaning money retreats, the second indicates legal problems, the third means bad luck – even going to jail – and the fourth indicates death of a spouse. (Pi: 2 1/8–4 1/4 ins, 54–108mm.)

LI: this category means separation and is similarly divided into four sub-sections. The first means a store of bad luck, the second predicts losing money, the third says you will meet up with unscrupulous people, and the fourth predicts being a victim of theft or burglary. (Li: 4 1/4–6 3/8 ins, 108–162mm.)

CHIEH: this category of bad dimension spells loss and has four sub-sections. The first spells death or departure of some kind, the second that everything you need will disappear and you could lose your livelihood, the third indicates you will be chased out of your village in disgrace, and the fourth indicates a very severe loss of money. (Chieh: 10 5/8–12 3/4 ins, 270–324mm.)

HAI: this fourth set of inauspicious dimensions indicates severe bad luck, starting with disasters arriving in the first sub-sector, death in the second, sicknesses and ill health in the third, and scandal and quarrels in the fourth. (Hai: 12 3/4–14 3/4 ins, 324–375mm.)

0mm

50

PI

100

LI

150

200

250

CHIEH

300

HAI

350

400

FORM SCHOOL
FENG SHUI

CONFIGURATION OF THE LANDSCAPE

The form school focuses on the configurations of the landscape, the presence of mountains and hills, waterways and lakes, the quality of the soil, and the wind, as well as the shapes and sizes of surrounding structures. Practicing landscape feng shui requires an understanding of animal symbolism because types of elevations are described as dragon or tiger hills or as turtle mountains and phoenix footstools. Elevations are also described in terms of the five elements (wood, fire, water, metal, and earth). Classical descriptions of good feng shui configurations have the mountain behind, preferably located north, the phoenix in front, preferably placed south and the dragon and the tiger curled in the form of an armchair.

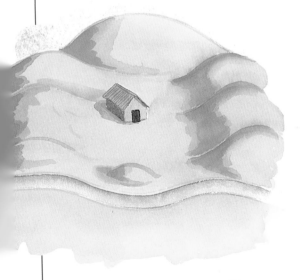

If your home is surrounded by hills in this manner, your family will be rich for generations. The dragon brings prosperity, the tiger protects you, the turtle assures you of longevity, and the phoenix brings you great opportunities. If there is also a river running in front of you, in full view of your front door, and it flows from left to right, you will be guaranteed enormous success in everything you undertake.

TOWNS AND CITIES

Hills and mountains can refer to buildings, and roads can take the place of rivers in town and city dwellers' analyses. Always ensure the following.

- ▧ Your main front door is not blocked by a large or tall building.
- ▧ The back of your building is protected by a taller or larger structure or hills in the distance.
- ▧ Buildings or raised ground on the left of your main door (looking out from inside) are higher than land on the right. The tiger must never be higher, otherwise it turns malevolent. If it is, install a bright spotlight high up on the left side of your main door.

THE TWO SCHOOLS

There are two major schools of feng shui practice. The form school looks at feng shui visually, diagnosing balance in terms of shape and form of the terrain. The compass school (see pages 34–39) takes a more precise view of orientation and direction and uses the compass extensively. Both schools are equally important and both methods should be used to get the best out of feng shui.

This house is situated where the hills to the right, the white tiger hills, are higher than those on the left, the green dragon hills. When the tiger is higher than the dragon it becomes malevolent rather than protective. However, its negative influences can be deflected by installing a very bright spotlight high up to the left of the front door.

~29~

GREEN DRAGONS, WHITE TIGERS, AND THE COSMIC BREATH

Classical feng shui talks about the green dragon and the white tiger, two of the four celestial animals used in landscape symbolism to assist practitioners to search out land sites that promise good luck. Dragons are never found where land is completely flat or where there are only jagged mountains – and where there is no dragon, the tiger, too, will be missing. Such locations are said to be extremely inauspicious.

Dragons and tigers are found where the land is gently undulating, the vegetation looks healthy and lush, the breezes are mild, the soil looks fertile, and the sunlight and shade are in balance. Such locations are extremely auspicious, but they are difficult to identify. A formation of hills alone seldom offers clear enough

indications and different types of high ground often exist side by side, making the search even harder. There are, however, some useful clues that you can look out for.

- Look for cloistered corners where the vegetation seems extra verdant.
- Feel the breeze and smell the air. If the wind is gentle and the air smells good, the dragon lives nearby.
- Look for places where there is both sunlight and shade.
- Dragons do not live on hilltops, where there is little protection. Avoid such sites.
- Dragons are not found where overhanging ridges and rocky outcrops threaten from above.
- Avoid land that is rocky and hard.
- Damp and musty places do not house dragons.

The dragon is always accompanied by the tiger. Identify them by seeing how the range of hills curves. Where two ranges meet, as if in an embrace, the site is deemed to be very special. This is where the dragon and the tiger are said to exude the greatest amount of cosmic breath, the sheng chi which brings extreme good fortune.

ENERGIZING THE CELESTIAL ANIMALS

The guidelines of dragon and tiger symbolism in landscape feng shui can be simulated indoors very simply. Place a painting or ceramic model of a dragon against the east wall of your living room to energize the auspicious dragon.

Let your main entrance door open into a small hall so that when the chi enters it has a chance to settle and not just rush away. Place turtles – real terrapins in an aquarium or ceramic models – in the north corner of your living room or behind your desk to symbolize the strong support of this celestial creature. Hang a picture of a glowing red phoenix in the south corner to bring opportunities your way.

The image of a dragon on the east wall of a room attracts the auspicious energy associated with this celestial animal.

The main premise of feng shui is to capture the auspicious chi of the dragon. Different parts of the dragon emit different quantities of chi, and feng shui is concerned with locating places in the landscape where it accumulates in abundance. These are areas that represent the dragon's heart and belly. The extremities of its body, such as the tail, are areas of stagnant chi. So a house built at the edge of elevated land, or on completely flat, low-lying land, will suffer from unsettled circumstances. There is no stability where the chi is tired.

Locations where the cosmic breath is scattered by high winds or carried away by fast-flowing rivers have no feng shui potential. Good luck cannot accumulate as chi evaporates before it can settle. A site is only auspicious when the flow of chi accumulates. Look for the following.

- Places where there are slow, meandering rivers.
- Places that are bordered by water.
- Places that are protected against harsh winds.
- Places where the surrounding hills are not too sharply pointed.

HILLS AND WATERCOURSES

There is also element significance in hills and watercourses. Their shapes and configurations, the way hills rise, and the way waters flow offer indications of their intrinsic element. Thus, there are water hills and fire waters and, depending on the ruling element of your year of birth, you can measure the degree of your personal affinity with the natural land forms and water that surround your own home.

TYPES OF HILL

Fire hills are conical in shape, rising up boldly, straight to a keen-edged, sharp point. Metal element people should not live near such hills, but those born in an earth year would benefit. However, this kind of hill directly facing the main door is disastrous for everyone.

Wood hills are round. They rise straight, have a long body, and are round at the summit. Those born in fire years are especially suited to living near such hills, but earth year people should avoid them. These hills are auspicious when they are behind the house.

Earth hills are square and look like plateaux with flat summits. They are excellent for those born during metal years, but are unsuitable for those whose element is water.

Water hills are ridged and appear to have several summits so that they look like a continuous range. Fire year people should not live near them, but wood element people will benefit from the affinity of energies with such a hill range.

Metal hills are oblong and are softly rounded, with a broad base and gentle slopes. These are suitable for those born during water years and are inauspicious for those born in wood years.

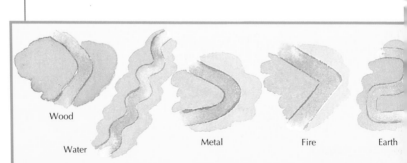

Wood

Water

Metal

Fire

Earth

INAUSPICIOUS SHAPES

Shapes that attract ill fortune are triangular, incomplete, and irregular. Other unlucky shapes are L- or U-shaped land and houses. Shapes that seem to have bits and pieces missing or jutting out are also deemed to be unbalanced and bring various different kinds of misfortunes, depending on which corners are missing and which jut out.

Missing corners can often be corrected by installing mirrors on walls, as these visually extend the corner. Alternatively, you can install a high, bright light in the missing corner which will serve to extend it symbolically.

Protruding corners appear like extensions to the basic shape with the result that other corners seem to be lacking. Since every corner of the home represents some kind of good fortune, these extensions can be auspicious or inauspicious depending on whether they are located in your personalized direction.

SHAPES

A selection of inauspicious shapes are shown here.

Regular shapes are always preferred to irregular shapes. So, for the purposes of feng shui, perfectly square or rectangular shapes are always deemed luckier than odd shapes. This is true for plots of land, houses, other buildings, rooms, windows, doors, and tables. Regular shapes are symmetrical and balanced; nothing is missing. For the practice of more advanced feng shui, which offers wonderful suggestions for energizing the various corners of a room or home, maximum benefit can be gained only when working with regular-shaped rooms. It is also easier to superimpose the Pa Kua and the Lo Shu square onto a regular-shaped room for additional feng shui analysis.

THE FLOW OF WATER

The angles made by flowing water are also described in terms of the five elements. If you live near a waterway or have drains around your home, check the suitability of the angles in relation to your personal year element, as well as to the element represented by the angle of the water. For example, angles in the north should ideally be of the water or metal element, in the south, of the fire or wood element and so forth.

~ 33 ~

COMPASS SCHOOL FENG SHUI

USING FORMULAS

Compass feng shui offers very precise use of formulas that spell out specific ways of investigating auspicious or inauspicious directions for orienting doors and entrances, the placement of furniture, and the direction for sleeping.

There are formulas to calculate individual auspicious and inauspicious directions based on personal Kua numbers and others for working out lucky and unlucky sectors of buildings from month to month and from year to year. The formulas address both the space and time dimensions of feng shui. They differentiate between east and west groups of people and buildings, offering methods for balancing personal energies with those of the environment. There are also formulas that address specific types of luck, particularly wealth luck, that have to do with the correct placement of water and its direction of flow around the living area.

Compass formula feng shui is a little more complex to learn than form school feng shui. However it is less subjective, which makes it easier to practice. Two of the formulas used in compass feng shui are given here.

AUSPICIOUS AND INAUSPICIOUS DIRECTIONS

1 — N: FW, NE: WK, E: TY, SE: SC, S: NY, SW: CM, W: HH, NW: LS

2 — N: CM, NE: SC, E: HH, SE: WK, S: LS, SW: FW, W: TY, NW: NY

3 — N: TY, NE: LS, E: FW, SE: NY, S: SC, SW: HH, W: CM, NW: WK

4 — N: SC, NE: CM, E: NY, SE: FW, S: TY, SW: WK, W: LS, NW: HH

9 — N: NY, NE: HH, E: SC, SE: CM, S: FW, SW: TY, W: WK, NW: CM

6 — N: LS, NE: TY, E: WK, SE: CM, S: NY, SW: SC, W: FW, NW: HH

7 — N: HH, NE: CM, E: NY, SE: LS, S: WK, SW: TY, W: FW, NW: SC

8 — N: WK, NE: FW, E: LS, SE: SC, S: HH, SW: NY, W: TY, NW: CM

THE KUA NUMBERS FORMULA

This is a powerfully potent method for discovering personalized auspicious and inauspicious directions based on birth dates. Calculate your Kua number as follows:

Check against the Chinese calendar (see pages 24-25) to make sure you use your Chinese year of birth.

Males
- Take your year of birth.
- Add the last two digits.
- If the result is more than 10, add the two digits to reduce them to a single number.
- Subtract from 10.
- **The answer is your Kua number.**

Example year of birth 1936:
3+6=9;
10-9=1
The Kua is 1.

Females
- Take your year of birth.
- Add the last two digits.
- If the result is more than 10, add the two digits to reduce them to a single number.
- Add 5.
- **The answer is your Kua number.**

Example year of birth 1945:
4+5=9;
9+5=14;
1+4=5
The Kua is 5.

The Kua numbers are the key to unlocking your auspicious and inauspicious directions. Kua numbers one, three, four, and nine have east, southeast, north, and south as the auspicious directions. The specific ranking of each of these directions and the precise type of luck they activate

Auspicious Locations	Inauspicious Locations
Fu Wei = FW	Ho Hai = HH
Tien Yi = TY	Wu Kwei = WK
Nien Yen = NY	Chueh Ming = CM
Sheng Chi = SC	Lui Sha = LS

for you make up the more detailed aspects of this formula and differ for each of the Kua numbers. It is sufficient to know that with these Kua numbers you are an east group person. The inauspicious directions for you are, therefore, the other four, the west group directions.

Kua numbers two, six, seven, and eight have west, southwest, northwest, and northeast as the auspicious directions. Again the specific ranking of each of these directions differs for each of the Kua numbers, but these are west group directions. The inauspicious directions for you are thus the other four, east group directions. There is no Kua number 5 in this system. Males who have a Kua number of 5 should use the number 2 and females who have a Kua number of 5 should use the number 8.

APPLYING THE
KUA NUMBERS FORMULA

Follow these suggestions for using Kua numbers for auspicious directions.

- ▨ Orientate your main door to face one of your auspicious directions.
- ▨ Work at a desk facing one of your auspicious directions.
- ▨ Sleep with your head pointing at one of your good directions.
- ▨ Eat, negotiate, give lectures, in other words undertake most activities, facing one of your best directions.
- ▨ Try to avoid having to do any of the above facing any of your inauspicious directions.

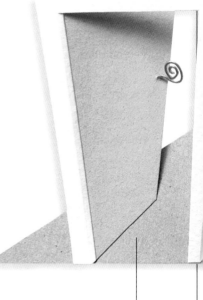

EXAMPLE

4

If your Kua number is **four**, you are an east group person and your auspicious directions are east, southeast, north, and south. These are the directions that you should face for your main and most important activities, as shown in the illustration here.

Orientate your door to face one of your best directions.

Always calculate the direction in which you should face by standing in the middle of the room and looking outward.

Select the seat in a meeting room or at the dining table at home that allows you to face one of your auspicious directions.

Sleep with your head pointing toward one of your best directions.

THE EIGHT LIFE ASPIRATIONS FORMULA

This formula is based on interpretations of the eight trigrams that are placed round the Later Heaven Pa Kua and is one of the easier compass theories to apply. Each side of the Pa Kua corresponds to a particular direction and is deemed to represent a specific kind of luck. Eight types of luck are identified and these are said to correspond to the sum total of humankind's aspirations. You will find, as you go deeper into feng shui, that the Chinese concept of luck is always expressed in terms of these particular eight aspirations.

- The attainment of wealth and prosperity.
- The attainment of a happy marriage.
- Getting respect, honor, and recognition.
- Longevity and good health.
- Having good descendants, that is, children and, specifically, sons.
- The attainment of education and knowledge.
- The help and support of influential people.
- Career promotions.

These aspirations can be specifically energized in several different ways that combine the use of other feng shui methods and formulas. Each of these eight types of luck is discussed in more comprehensive detail in the other books in this series. As an introduction to the method, however, it is useful to study the illustrated Pa Kua here that provides the basic formula.

Sun
South-east
Wealth and prosperity

Chen
East
Family relationships and health

Ken
North-east
Education

Li
South
Recognition and fame

Kun
South-west
Marriage prospects and marital happiness

Tui
West
Luck of children

Kan
North
Career prospects

Chien
North-west
Presence of helpful people or mentors

POISON ARROWS AND THE KILLING BREATH

THE KILLING BREATH

Bad feng shui is almost always caused by what is termed the killing breath, or shar chi, and every school of feng shui repeatedly warns against being hit by the shar chi of secret poison arrows within the environment that bring this deadly and pernicious energy. These usually come in the form of straight lines, sharp angles, or anything that is shaped this way. When pointed in a threatening manner at your home, especially at your front door, the result is extreme bad luck, loss, and ill health. In some cases the poison arrows can even bring death to the unfortunate residents of the house.

When practicing feng shui it is advisable to start by taking a defensive posture to guard against the killing breath. Only then should you turn your attention to harnessing good chi flows. Remember that, even if you have the best dragon and tiger configurations and irrespective of all your orientations being auspicious, a single deadly arrow can spoil everything.

The straight lines of this row of poplar trees can, in some situations, act like poison arrows directing the killing breath toward your home.

OTHER EXAMPLE

Sharp edge of a building   A dead tree tru

POISON ARROWS

Poison arrows that cause shar chi can be any hostile, threatening, or imposing structure whose energies overwhelm the energies of your home. They can also be straight hill ridges, the angle of a roof line, the edge of a building, or a straight road or river.

THE T-JUNCTION

If the front door of your house faces a T-junction, as shown here, or any other offending structure, you can protect yourself against the killing breath in one of several ways.

▨ Re-orientate or move your main door so that the bad energy is deflected.

▨ Plant a row of trees with good foliage so that the oncoming road is 'blocked off'.

▨ Build a wall that effectively closes off the view of the offending road.

▨ Hang a Pa Kua with a mirror outside above the center of the door to ward off the shar chi and prevent it from entering your home.

F POISON ARROWS

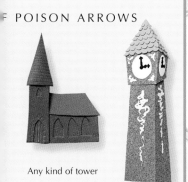

Any kind of tower

A mirror will deflect shar chi away from your home

~41~

LOOKING OUT FOR ARROWS

Unless you deliberately become aware of your surroundings, it is easy to miss hostile structures that could well be sending harmful energies your way. Looking out for poison arrows requires practice. Just remember that anything sharp, pointed, angular, or hostile has the potential to harm you if it is directed toward your door.

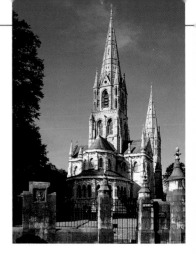

- ❖ A common cause of shar chi is the triangular shape of the roof lines of a neighbor's house. If such a structure is facing you, try to re-orient your door.
- ❖ Living near to or facing electrical transmitters or pylons often causes negative energies to build up. Shield them from view by growing a clump of trees between them and your home.

- ❖ Directly facing a church, any kind of steeple, or a huge cross is inauspicious. Reflect back any negative vibrations with a Pa Kua mirror.

Other examples of structures that can emanate poisonous or killing breath at your home include signboards and pointers, windmills, sharp hills, tall buildings, cannons, and tree trunks. Remember that they are harmful from a feng shui viewpoint only if they are directly hitting, or facing, the main front door of your house.

- ❖ A highway overpass that resembles blades hitting the front of your home also causes imbalance. Move away from such a house or building or hang a large wind chime between the overpass and your door.

Certain features in your surroundings, like sharp mountains (right), have the potential to create problems for you if their harmful energies are pointed directly at your main front door.

~42~

OBJECTS CAN DEFLECT POISON ARROWS

When dealing with poison arrows, try to match the element of the object used as a cure with the compass location where there is a problem. Listed here are six such objects that can be used to deal with poison arrows.

WIND CHIMES

They are often excellent for countering the ill effects of protrusions from ceilings and structural beams. Metal wind chimes are especially effective when they are hung in the west and northwest corners of rooms.

PLANTS

These are excellent for shielding and dissolving shar chi, especially when placed against corners. As they also symbolize growth, they are perfect feng shui when placed in the east corners of rooms.

SCREENS

These are extremely popular with the Chinese as they are good at blocking energy that is moving too fast. By slowing down the pernicious breath, screens transform harmful energy into auspicious energy.

DRAPES

These are very effective when used to block out bad views of threatening structures that create shar chi. Use heavy drapes or chintz curtains. They are effective in any corner of the home, but select colors according to the elements of the corners. Use red for the south, dark blue for the north, green for the east, and white for the west.

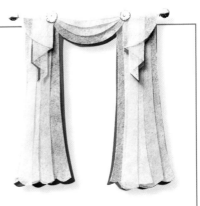

MIRRORS

These are powerful feng shui tools because their reflective quality has the effect of sending shar chi to back where it came from. Mirrors also widen narrow, cramped corners and extend walls to make up for missing corners. However, they should be used carefully. They must not reflect the main door, nor should they reflect toilets. Mirrors are auspicious in dining rooms but should not reflect the bed of the master bedroom.

LIGHTS

These are powerful antidotes for all kinds of feng shui problems. They are especially good when used to dissolve the shar chi of sharp edges and protruding corners, particularly when placed in the south corners of rooms, except angular lights like this which are not beneficial.

DEALING WITH ARROWS INSIDE THE HOME

It is also necessary to watch out for poison arrows inside the home. Shar chi is usually created when there are sharp edges caused by furniture, protruding corners, individual square pillars, and exposed overhead beams. Being hit by the sharp edges of these structures causes migraine and other illnesses and, in severe cases, it can also bring bad luck in the form of unexpected financial and career loss.

Block off the sharp edge of a protruding corner with a large plant as shown here.

Dissolve the shar chi of individual square pillars by covering them with mirrors that effectively make them disappear.

Placing crystals at the edge of a sharp protruding corner will deflect shar chi.

Deal with exposed overhead beams by hanging two flutes, tied with red thread and positioned diagonally.

Alternatively, hang a wind chime to soften the shar chi emanating from a beam.

Open book shelves are bad feng shui. They act like blades, cutting at residents. It is always preferable to have doors.

FENG SHUI TIPS
FOR INTERIORS

RESIDENTIAL ROOM LAYOUTS

Good feng shui starts with the main door, which should open outward to an empty space, termed the bright hall, where the cosmic chi can settle and accumulate before entering your home. It should also lead into a space that is not too cramped. This allows chi to gather before meandering through your home.

MAIN DOOR TABOOS

- ▨ The main door should never open into a cramped hall. Install a bright light if the space is too narrow.
- ▨ The main door should never open directly into a staircase. Place a screen in between or curve the bottom of the stairs.
- ▨ There should not be a toilet too near the main door. This causes chi that enters the home to become sour.

Well-lit and clean apartments attract auspicious energies. Small, dark, and unused corners create killing breath, so air store rooms occasionally. Do not have too many doors opening from a long corridor; this will cause quarrels. The ratio of windows to doors should not exceed 3:1. Doors should not directly face a window, as chi will come in and go out again.

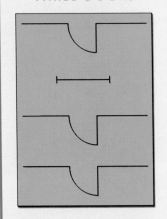

THREE DOORS

Three doors in a straight line are deadly feng shui. The chi is moving too fast. Hang a wind chime or place a dividing screen in front of the middle door.

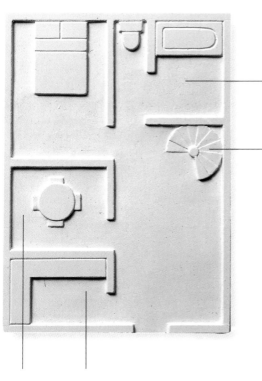

Toilets and bathrooms should not be located in the north corner of the home, as this flushes away career and promotion opportunities for the breadwinner.

Staircases should ideally be curved and winding. Spiral staircases resemble a corkscrew and are harmless when placed in a corner, but deadly when located in the middle of the home.

Rooms should be regular in shape, with kitchens located in the back half of the home.

Dining areas should be higher than living rooms if there are split levels.

The ideal arrangement of rooms will encourage chi to move smoothly through your home.

Good room location at the far corner of the office building.

If you take care over the feng shui of your office, your business will prosper.

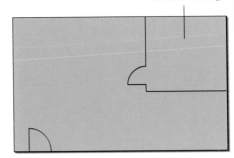

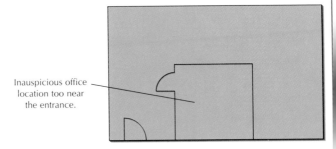

Inauspicious office location too near the entrance.

OFFICE FENG SHUI

When you have good feng shui at work there is harmony in the office and co-operative spirit prevails. Bad feng shui can lead to discord and collapsing profits. If you are in a managerial position, your room should ideally be located deep inside the office, but not at the end of a long corridor. The fortunes of the entire office are affected by your feng shui.

- ▨ Regular-shaped rooms are always to be preferred over odd-shaped rooms.
- ▨ All protruding corners should be camouflaged with plants.
- ▨ Avoid sitting directly below an overhead beam.
- ▨ If a window opens to a view of a sharp angle, keep it permanently closed.
- ▨ Do not sit directly facing open book shelves.

SITTING DIRECTIONS

Never sit with your back to the door. You will literally be stabbed in the back. Do not sit with your back to the window. You will lack support for your suggestions and ideas. Always sit facing the door at whatever angle you like and ideally facing one of your good luck directions, according to compass feng shui. Whatever your sitting position and direction, make sure it does not seem awkward. Do not attempt to sit facing your best compass direction if in the process you get stabbed by a poison arrow caused by the arrangement of the office furniture or an individual pillar.

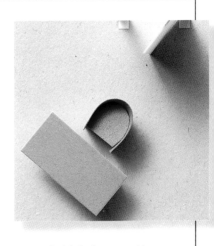

Bad desk placement with the back to the door.

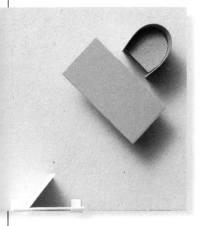

Good desk placement. The desk faces the door. Place a painting or print of a mountain behind the desk to symbolize support.

Never sit too near the door; you will be easily distracted.

ARRANGING FURNITURE

Living room furniture should never be L-shaped. Try to simulate the Pa Kua shape when arranging a lounge suite and coffee table, as this is conducive to creating good social interactions between those sitting there. It is a good idea to find your favorite place when entertaining friends.

It should be one of your auspicious compass directions. Place the television and stereo on the west or northwest side and a pot plant or some flowers on the east side of the room. The fireplace should ideally be located in the south, but is also acceptable to situate it in the southwest or northeast.

The television and stereo should ideally be in the west or northwest of the room.

The fireplace should be in the northeast, southwest, or south.

The room where people gather should encourage harmony.

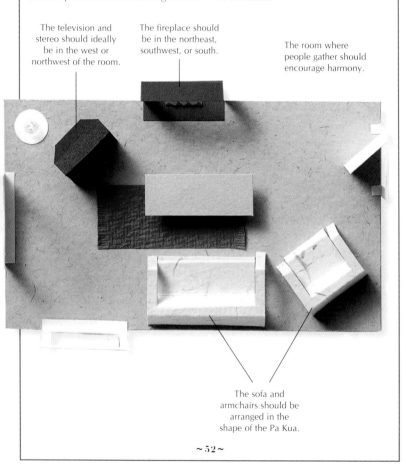

The sofa and armchairs should be arranged in the shape of the Pa Kua.

Good bed placement.

Peaceful and refreshing sleep will be guaranteed if the beds are well placed.

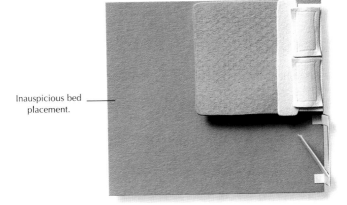

Inauspicious bed placement.

BEDROOMS

Bedrooms must have good bed arrangements. Place the bed diagonally opposite the door and do not sleep with your feet directly pointed toward it, as this is deemed the death position. Do not sleep under an overhead beam. Do not have mirrors directly facing the bed, as this is extremely inauspicious. While plants generally represent good feng shui, it is not advisable to have them in bedrooms. The yang energy of plants can sometimes disturb the yin energies required for a good night's sleep.

FENG SHUI TIPS
FOR EXTERIORS

CHANNELLING
VIBRANT EARTH ENERGIES

風
水

One of the most effective ways of channeling healthy earth energy for the home is to introduce auspicious feng shui features into the garden. No matter how small your garden may be, if the directions are conducive to introducing specific feng shui activators, it is advisable to do so. There are some easy ways of doing this.

- ▨ Introduce a garden light if the garden has a south orientation.
- ▨ Introduce a small fountain if it has a north orientation.
- ▨ Build a low brick wall if it is southwest.

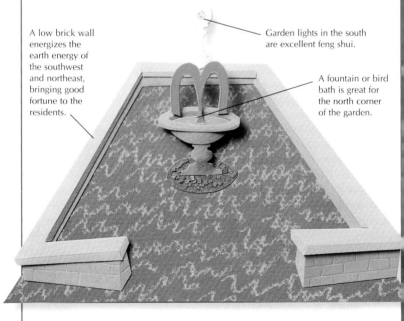

A low brick wall energizes the earth energy of the southwest and northeast, bringing good fortune to the residents.

Garden lights in the south are excellent feng shui.

A fountain or bird bath is great for the north corner of the garden.

Place terrapins in a small trough of water and feed
them regularly or display a fake model of a turtle
above a small mound of earth in your garden.
This should attract good fortune into your home.

Another great way of channeling energy from the ground is to sink a long, hollow pole deep into the ground and place a round light at the top. This encourages auspicious sheng chi to rise and residents enjoy good fortune from this positive energy.

LONGEVITY AND GOOD HEALTH WITH THE TURTLE

Another particularly good tip for the outdoors is to introduce the symbol of longevity in the form of the celestial turtle. Placed in the north part of the garden, real turtles bring exceptionally good luck, but a ceramic model will do just as well. The turtle is symbolic of heavenly luck in the form of good health, protection, and support.

BALANCE IS EVERYTHING

Do not expect overnight success. Be patient and make subtle adjustments when necessary. If you harness and channel earth energy in your home and environment, good fortune will follow.

INDEX

FURTHER READING

Kwok, Man-Ho and O'Brien, Joanne,
The Elements of Feng Shui,
ELEMENT BOOKS, SHAFTESBURY, 1991

Lo, Raymond *Feng Shui: The Pillars of
Destiny (Understanding Your Fate and
Fortune),* TIMES EDITIONS, SINGAPORE, 1995

Skinner, Stephen *Living Earth Manual
of Feng Shui: Chinese Geomancy,*
PENGUIN, 1989

Too, Lillian *Basic Feng Shui,* KONSEP BOOKS,
KUALA LUMPUR, 1997

Too, Lillian *Chinese Astrology for Romance
& Relationships,* KONSEP BOOKS,
KUALA LUMPUR, 1996

Too, Lillian *Chinese Numerology
in Feng Shui,* KONSEP BOOKS,
KUALA LUMPUR, 1994

Too, Lillian *Dragon Magic,* KONSEP BOOKS,
KUALA LUMPUR, 1996

Too, Lillian *The Complete Illustrated Guide
to Feng Shui,* ELEMENT BOOKS,
SHAFTESBURY, 1996

Too, Lillian *Feng Shui,* KONSEP BOOKS,
KUALA LUMPUR, 1993

Too, Lillian *Practical Applications for
Feng Shui,* KONSEP BOOKS,
KUALA LUMPUR, 1994

Too, Lillian *Water Feng Shui for Wealth,*
KONSEP BOOKS, KUALA LUMPUR, 1995

Walters, Derek *Feng Shui Handbook:
A Practical Guide to Chinese Geomancy
and Environmental Harmony,*
AQUARIAN PRESS, 1991

USEFUL ADDRESSES

Feng Shui Design Studio
PO Box 705, Glebe, Sydney, NSW 2037,
Australia, Tel: 61 2 315 8258

Feng Shui Society of Australia
PO Box 1565, Rozelle, Sydney
NSW 2039, Australia

The Geomancer
The Feng Shui Store
PO Box 250, Woking, Surrey GU21 1YJ
Tel: 44 1483 839898
Fax: 44 1483 488998

Feng Shui Association
31 Woburn Place, Brighton BN1 9GA,
Tel/Fax: 44 1273 693844

Feng Shui Network International
PO Box 2133, London W1A 1RL,
Tel: 44 171 935 8935,
Fax: 44 171 935 9295

The School of Feng Shui
34 Banbury Road, Ettington,
Stratford-upon-Avon, Warwickshire
CV37 7SU. Tel/Fax: 44 1789 740116

The Feng Shui Institute of America
PO Box 488, Wabasso, FL 32970,
Tel: 1 407 589 9900 Fax: 1 407 589 1611

Feng Shui Warehouse
PO Box 3005, San Diego, CA 92163,
Tel: 1 800 399 1599 Fax: 1 800 997 9831

**Other titles in the
Feng Shui Fundamentals
series are:**

Careers
Children
Education
Fame
Health
Love
Networking
Wealth